THE SEVEN D's
OF GREAT LEADERSHIP

THE SEVEN D's
OF GREAT LEADERSHIP

Dr. Jimmie A. Ellis, III

All Scripture quotations unless otherwise marked are taken from The New King James Version of the Holy Bible. Copyright © 1979, 1980, 1982, Thomas Nelson, Inc., Publishers.

Publishing services by Selah Publishing Group, LLC, Tennessee. The views expressed or implied in this work do not necessarily reflect those of Selah Publishing Group.

ISBN: 978-1-58930-238-9
Library of Congress Control Number: 2009903946

This book is dedicated to all of those who have sacrificed their lives in helping their leaders and at the same time investing in their own future.

No one knows the cost you have paid to stand where you are.

Someone understands.

Dr. Jimmie A. Ellis, III

M.O.G. (Man of God)

Contents

Introduction

I have been in ministry my entire life. In that time, I have served the church in many ways including:

- ◆ Ushers/Greeters – Department Head
- ◆ Choir Director – (5 different choirs)

I understand church service inside and out and have come to realize that one must first learn to be a great follower (sheep) before he can become a great leader (shepherd).

I have developed 7 D's of great leadership that I want to outline in this book.

This is a true saying, if a man desire the office of a bishop, he desireth a great work.
1 TIMOTHY 3:1

The Makings
of a Great Leader

1. Desire

Desire is the fuel that lights the fire and motivates us to act. There are many saints who are content to simply attend service, hear a great Word, and go home. They have no "desire" to serve and we make a mistake when we attempt to recruit them. Perhaps there was a time in your own life when you were not motivated to serve. You did not want to get involved in ministry because you did not want God meddling in your business. But God began to change your desires and you found that you "had" to get involved. You developed a desire to work for God and help others and you were motivated to attend church and render service even when you weren't feeling well or didn't have money.

Desire can be detected in our body language. Your pastor can determine if you truly wish to work in the church simply by reading your body language. The best way to recruit workers for your ministry is to pursue those who attend church regularly. The fact that they are consistent in church attendance proves that they have desire and are motivated.

Those who have desire are also:

- *Hungry*
  Blessed are they which do hunger and thirst after righteousness: for they shall be filled.
  MATTHEW 5:6
- *Seeking*
  I love them that love me; and those that seek me early shall find me.
  PROVERBS 8:17

  And ye shall seek me, and find me, when ye shall search for me with all your heart. And I will be found of you, saith the LORD:
  JEREMIAH 29:13-14A

Desire is a phenomenon that cannot be explained and you either have or you do not. Do not waste time trying to explain your desire to someone who cannot understand. Your great love for God will motivate you to do things that others will not understand. Those who have no knowledge or love for God will not understand your desire to serve Him. Love for God will motivate us to serve even when we are not paid. It will be easy to distinguish between those who are in it just for the money as opposed to those who are in it for the vision. Those who are in it just for the money will fade away when the money isn't forthcoming. Those who are in it for the vision will report for duty with or without being paid.

There will be times when you will have to work with people who are not fully qualified for the job. Jesus worked with people who were not as competent as He was. He said,

> **And Jesus said unto them, Come ye after me, and I will make you to become fishers of men.**
> **MARK 1:17**

People who have desire will do ministry without receiving payment for their time and expertise. In some cases, payment may come later. Doing ministry voluntarily will confirm whether the person is working for the vision or for the money. None of the disciples followed Jesus for money. The disciples believed in Jesus' vision and were motivated by desire. Jesus also accepted them even though they were not as competent as He was. In Matthew 4:19, Jesus said, *Follow me and I will make you fishers of men.* Why did Jesus pick people who were less competent than He was? It was because they had the desire to be developed, dependable, daring and duplicated.

People who have desire are passionate. It is wise to get your eyes off of the people who do not come to church. Get your eyes off of the empty seats and begin to look at the seats that are full. The vision is caught by those who are not absent from church.

It is possible for people to give to your ministry and not catch your vision. These types of persons value their giving as a donation and they are not committed to give. When you are committed, you must give. Tithes and offerings are in the same category as paying your electric bill and your gas bill. You do not decide that your bills will not get paid. Therefore, you should not contemplate whether you are going to tithe or not. Tithing is complete because you are bound to the ministry that you are connected to. Never give to a ministry that you are not connected to and are not being fed by consistently. If you find yourself giving to an outside ministry more than your home church, you might want to consider moving your membership to that ministry. The intentions of your heart are revealed through the way you spend your money.

There is nothing wrong with supporting other ministries but your own church should **always** have priority over any outside ministry. You should always give where your meals are prepared, served and consumed. If you happen to eat meals at other ministries, always remember that you are munching on a snack not savoring a meal.

A sure sign that you have drifted toward the flesh is a decrease in your desire for the things of God. Your fire and desire are connected. Be careful when you feel a decrease in desire for your ministry. We all experience a slacking off of desire. This does not mean that we are bad people. The great news is that despite low ebb in our desire, God will continue to flow until our desire begins to peak again.

Trials and tribulations can cause us to experience a downturn in our desire. When a downturn happens to you, the best thing to do is seek advice from your pastor or leader. Turn to your pastor and make him aware of your situation so that he can pray for you. Remember, the enemy uses trials and tribulations to decrease your effectiveness. Satan's operations must be exposed so he can be defeated.

Our effectiveness in ministry is adversely affected when we fail to expose the enemy's work in our lives. We begin to lose our passion for ministry because we have been deceived into viewing the situation through our flesh (while in the trial) rather than through the Spirit of God. When we are facing a trial we may begin to believe that no one cares. We begin to wonder why others have not been able to discern (notice through their spirit) that we are suffering. Do not wait for others to approach you. Seek out people who can advise you. Do not play games.

Be open about your problems. Remember, the enemy seeks to destroy your desire (passion), and if he fails in that effort, he will attack the fuel that ignites your desire.

2. Development

When something "develops" it grows progressively into a higher form. As you develop your leadership skills, you must grow in wisdom (teaching) and stature (training). Stature is defined as "height". You grow from one height level to another.

> **And Jesus increased in wisdom and stature, and in favour with God and man.**
>
> **LUKE 2:25**

◆ *Wisdom*

Wisdom comes through instruction received from the Man of God or your department head. If you expect to increase in your level of development you must respect your department head just as you respect your Pastor. The department head has been given the same anointing as the Man of God – the anointing flows down from the head. When you have a problem, follow the chain of command and seek out your department head first. Give him (or her) due respect. The mere fact that the Pastor has chosen him (or her) for that role proves that the Pastor has confidence in them.

> **And he goeth up into a mountain, and calleth unto him whom he would: and they came unto him. And he ordained twelve, that they should be with him, and that he might send them forth to preach,**
>
> **MARK 3:13-14**

It is vital that you have the spirit of the House. You get the spirit of the House by receiving the teaching and training found there. The 12 disciples received the Spirit of Jesus because they were "with" Him. To grow and develop in leadership requires commitment. Commitment means you will attend church, despite being tired. Commitment means you will serve during the week when only 20 people are in attendance with the same fervor as you do on Sunday.

Jesus called the 12 so they could receive His teachings. You develop the spirit of the House by attending services. A note to members who have transferred from other churches, you cannot bring the teachings of your former church to your new church. You must acquire the spirit of the new church and flow with it.

♦ *Stature*

Stature is defined as development, growth, or level of attainment, especially as worthy of esteem.

> **After these things the LORD appointed other seventy also, and sent them two and two before his face into every city and place, whither he himself would come.**
> **LUKE 10:1**
> **And the seventy returned again with joy, saying, Lord, even the devils are subject unto us through thy name.**
> **LUKE 10:17**

Jesus had instructed the 70 to do something they had never done before. They had never before cast out a devil. I am pointing this out because many of you sell yourselves short. You only want to do something if you feel confident in your abilities. But, if the Pastor asks you to do something you have not done before, you resist. When you sell yourself short, you are rejecting the gift that is hidden within you. God will stretch us by having us do things that are unfamiliar and it takes a Man of God, with discernment, to bring that hidden gift to the forefront. The Helps Ministry is designed to reveal hidden gifts!!!

You experience growth in ministry when you actually go out and "do" something. Some people think that they are being trained when they attend church and receive the Word. This is not the case; you are merely receiving nuggets of Truth. You discover what you can do by going out and doing something. One of my Knights was a Muslim before he joined my church. He came through the ranks seeking the assurance that he could indeed serve in his current capacity as one of my Knights. Through actual service, going out and "doing" it, he has matured in a way that he could not have by receiving teaching alone.

When you are under teaching, you are simply submitting your "ears", but when you are being "trained", you must submit your mouth, hands, and feet. You will never know if you can teach if you are never challenged. You may feel insecure at first, but once the anointing falls upon you, you will move forward and grow in stature.

Perhaps you are wondering why your Pastor is asking you to do so much. You may be wondering "why is the Pastor giving me all of this to do?" Pastors are able to see things that you are not able to see. I understand that you will be nervous when called upon to do a new thing, but I want to encourage you to make the transition from the old to the new. When we advance into new areas it is understandable that we will feel fearful. That's why when God has a new thing for us He says "fear not".

Jesus took His disciples through 4 different stages of development:

- ◆ **Stage 1: Come & See**
  In John 1, Andrew told Peter that Jesus had arrived and that he should "come & see" Him.
- ◆ **Stage 2: Come & Follow**
  Jesus tells Peter and the other disciples to follow Him and He would make them fishers of men.

- ◆ ***Stage 3: Come & Commit***
  Jesus said, "If you love Me and hate not your father, your mother, your wife and your children, then you cannot be My disciple. Pick up your cross and follow Me."

- ◆ ***Stage 4: Come & Multiply***
  This is the stage of maturity. Jesus told His disciples to go out and duplicate themselves.

If you have decided to be in Helps Ministry, you are at Stage 3. This is where you will be tested. Church attendance is "come & see"; responding to the altar call is "come & follow"; and becoming involved in ministry is "come & commit". When you commit, you experience the reward of "come & multiply (duplicate)". God will transform you from a sheep to a shepherd.

Everyone gets excited about the Five-Fold ministry, but they do not realize that development is required. When a prophet or Man of God prophesies over you, he is declaring the end from the beginning, but that does not mean that you are at your end. There are additional steps involved.

3. Dependability

You are dependable when others can count on you. Dependability means you are faithful and can be trusted to handle an assignment. Faithfulness and dependability are required of great stewards.

**Moreover it is required in stewards,
that a man be found faithful.**
1 CORINTHIANS 4:2

A steward is the person hired to manage the property or day-to day affairs of someone else. The steward is literally "one over a house," one charged with oversight of household operations.

Remember, the department that you manage does not "belong" to you. This is a major problem with churches in our culture. Many who assume a position begin to think that they are the "king" of the position. As result, a spirit of witchcraft is birthed in the church and people attempt to control and manipulate others. Do not forget that you are only a "steward" managing what belongs to someone else. You are not irreplaceable and God will replace you if you get high-minded and arrogant.

Pastors, don't ever think that you are so anointed that you can not be replaced. If God can fire Saul, everyone can be fired. This is what should keep you humbled. Your gift should not make you conceited! Be watchful because every rocket has a launching pad. Don't forget your launching pad! If it were not for the launching pad, the rocket would have never been able to take off. You will be tested when you are receiving more offers for speaking engagements or to preach. There is nothing wrong with accepting an offer to speak; just make sure that it is not on a night when you should be at your own church!

Here are words of wisdom to those serving under a pastor: If you desire to accept a speaking engagement, make sure you first get permission from your pastor. You will surely be located if you are told "no". God is trying to keep you level-headed. The pastor is not trying to control you. These are the thoughts that never come to mind when you do not know what your gift is. A good pastor will not hold you back. He will let you go. He will see your maturity and discern when you are not ready to be launched. Just because a baby knows how to walk does not mean that he knows

how to change his diapers. When the Man of God
tells you that he does not want you to go to a cer-
tain place, it may also be because he may have spe-
cial knowledge about the church that has extended
the invitation and it may not be appropriate to go.
Trust your pastor's judgment.

4. Daring

To be daring means to be bold in thought or action. In Matthew 14:28, when Jesus walked on the water, Peter said, "Lord, if it is you, bid me to come." Peter was daring. He was willing to do that which normal people would not.

If you work in the Helps Ministry, stop seeing yourself as normal. Those who serve in this capacity are "above" average in the Kingdom of God because the average person is not willing to do much. There is a great deal of talking in the Kingdom of God; but very little action. If you are going to be daring, expect to be talked about. Daring people are always talked about. Taking charge is not for the faint of heart because daring people:

A. Initiate

When you initiate things you are not supposed to wait for others, you take the lead in activating something. This means you come to meetings armed with ideas. When you take the initiative you will meet with the pastor to discuss plans for improving your department. You do not wait for the pastor to tell "you" what should be done. You will see what needs to be done and develop your own ideas.

B. Are Decisive

Being decisive means you have the ability to make decisions. The ability to make great decisions is very important for a department head. Many people, however, are reluctant to make decisions because they do not want to be held responsible should their plans fail. News Flash: there is no authority without responsibility. If you have been named the captain of a ship, it is your responsibility to instruct the people in the steering of that ship. You cannot call yourself a leader if you are unwilling to make decisions. If your pastor has to make decisions for you, then you have failed in your role as a leader.

As a church leader, it is your duty to protect the church. As a result, you may have to release someone from a ministry. A great leader will have the strength to make the decision and inform the person being affected. You should be able to say "I" made this decision. Do not fall into the trap of attempting to shift blame to the pastor by saying "Pastor said…". Have the courage to demonstrate your authority and boldly state that "I" made this decision.

C. Exercise Authority

When you are in authority, you must exercise that authority with confidence so that it will not be usurped. Your staff will know by your actions that you take authority seriously.

D. Have Courage

Having courage means you have the mental and moral strength to withstand opposition. You may still be in contact with people that you had to release from ministry. Have the courage to interact with them even if they seem to want to avoid you. Continue to demonstrate the love of Christ. It is important that you both realize that the decision to release them from ministry was a "business" decision not based on any personal attitudes.

In your role as a leader you may have to make adverse decisions that affect your friends. Be prepared for those who will only want to be your friend because of your leadership position. Be careful about how you relate to others. It's okay to let people "touch" you, but do not let them "feel" you. When you allow a person to "feel" you, it may be difficult to go against them when the time comes to make a decision that may be against what they "think is right". Be wise in associating with others.

5. Duplicate

You are responsible for stimulating growth in your ministry. Duplicate yourself by delegating responsibility to those who serve in your ministry. Your staff is not there just to watch you do all the work. They are there to participate in the work required to sustain and grow the ministry. Test the faithfulness of your staff by assigning responsibilities without titles. You will know who is not suitable to handle additional responsibility by their attitude and response. Those who constantly complain are not suited for responsibilities or titles.

How can you know when you have been successful in duplicating yourself? You will know when your ministry is able to function even when you are absent. You will be able to take a vacation and be assured that the ministry will function as well as if you were on hand personally. Make sure you place trustworthy individuals in leadership roles. When you are unavailable, these persons should be able to manage the department, report on activities, and resolve any problems that may arise. These persons will always place the viability of the department over and above their personal friendships. They will not show favoritism, but operate in the best interest of the ministry.

6. Devotion

It is a heavy burden to sacrifice for people who do not appreciate the sacrifice. It hurts when we demonstrate love and that love is not reciprocated. It can be quite a challenge to continue in ministry when this happens. Devotion comes in when you are challenged to manage your own personal difficulties in addition to those you are handling for the church.

> As for the sons of Merari, thou shalt
> number them after their families, by
> the house of their fathers; From
> thirty years old and upward even
> unto fifty years old shalt thou num-
> ber them, every one that entereth into
> the service, to do the work of the tab-
> ernacle of the congregation. And this
> is the charge of their burden, accord-
> ing to all their service in the taber-

nacle of the congregation; the boards of the tabernacle, and the bars thereof, and the pillars thereof, and sockets thereof, And the pillars of the court round about, and their sockets, and their pins, and their cords, with all their instruments, and with all their service: and by name ye shall reckon the instruments of the charge of their burden.

NUMBERS 4:29-32

From thirty years old and upward even unto fifty years old, every one that came to do the service of the ministry, and the service of the burden in the tabernacle of the congregation.

NUMBERS 4:47

The word "burden" means "responsibility". Responsibility can be a burden. To put it in today's vernacular, ministry can stress you out. If you wish to work in ministry, you MUST have a CONSISTENT prayer life. This is where many in ministry fail. If you have a weak prayer life, you will not succeed in ministry. Great pastors are enabled to do what they do because they have strong prayer lives. It takes much more than simply knowing the Word to survive in ministry. Having a strong prayer life strengthens you and prepares you to handle the rigors of ministry. You should pray until God's presence saturates your very soul.

Come unto me, all ye that labour and are heavy laden, and I will give you rest. Take my yoke upon you, and learn of me; for I am meek and lowly in heart: and ye shall find rest unto your souls.
MATTHEW 11:28-29

Having a consistent prayer life will defeat all the temptations of the flesh. Most of us tend to fall into sin during stressful situations. But when we have a healthy prayer life, the power of God will sustain us when we are tempted to sin.

And the people murmured against Moses, saying, What shall we drink? And he cried unto the LORD; and the LORD shewed him a tree, which when he had cast into the waters, the waters were made sweet:
EXODUS 15:24-25A

Moses had a very strong AND consistent prayer life. When he was assailed from every side, he cried out to the Lord. People "will" test your patience and you will be tempted to leave ministry. When this happens, just remember "why" you are in ministry and "Who" you are really serving.

Many believers will fall away from the church when they begin working behind the scenes and see the true personalities of those in ministry. They will discover that some in leadership are not as holy or nice as they appear to be in public. It will be revealed that some leaders' bad habits will come to surface as they give in to temptation and sin. When this situation arise (and it will), do not be discouraged. Continue to love the individual with a mature attitude even though the leader's idiosyncracies are evident. Mature Christians will know that God's anointing may still be upon the church despite the leader's weaknesses. Pray for the leader. This will empower you to look beyond the faults of the leader and see the needs of God's people.

7. Discipline

Discipline is defined as being obedient, having restraint, control and order. When you are working for God, you must have discipline in your personal life. If you do not have discipline, the enemy will be able to gain a stronghold in your life and become a distraction.

Many people lose their anointing to serve in the church because they become so enamored with "performance" that they forget to "minister". If you are not living righteously before the Lord, you will be unable to minister to the people of God. If you fail or make a mistake, ask God to forgive you, clean up your act, and return to your duties. If you find that you are truly struggling in an area of weakness, seek the counsel of your pastor or other trusted leader. Make your pastor or other trusted leader aware of your situation so they can stand in the gap for you and pray for your victory. This is the best way to defeat the enemy.

To be a great leader, you must allow God to consecrate the gift that He put inside you. Whether you are a pastor, department head, or serving on the Helps Ministry, spend time with God in prayer and worship so that you may be able to hear from Him when He speaks. Having a gift and the anointing means you must take time to be fresh and vibrant so that both may manifest 100% through you. When you put these things to practice, there is no doubt that God will show up because He honors your diligence and faithfulness. God will honor the fact that when no one was looking, you disciplined yourself; not to receive accolades and recognition from people but because in your heart you desire to be the Man (or Woman) of God that He purposed you to be.

About the Author

In 1985, Dr. Ellis founded Arnaz Ministries School of the Word Bible Institute. As Founder and President, Dr. Ellis designed a curriculum to train individuals who've been called to a five-fold ministry, the ministry of counseling, and those who desire an in-depth study of the Word of God for spiritual fulfillment. Today, the two-year program offers a variety of selective and innovative courses conducive to developing church leaders of all facets.

In 1999, Dr. Ellis founded The Conquerors Community Development Corporation (CCDC), a mission designed to elevate the quality of life for the Southwest Philadelphia community through economic development, child development, technological awareness, spiritual/cultural programs and health initiatives. Dr. Ellis' vision is to further institute employment services, daycare services, housing and community revitalization programs, health related projects and life skills to empower the community.

In March 2004, Dr. Ellis received his honorary Doctorate of Divinity Degree from Saint Thomas Christian College in Jacksonville, Florida. Dr. Ellis' contributions have been applauded throughout the city by the media, governing officials and with numerous awards.

To order additional copies of

THE SEVEN D's
OF GREAT LEADERSHIP

have your credit card ready and call
1 800-917-BOOK (2665)

or e-mail
orders@selahbooks.com

or order online at
www.selahbooks.com

Printed in the United States
144102LV00001B/3/P